Lib. En. Bks 09
20.00

D1302968

OPELIKA HIGH LIBRARY

Documenting World War II

The Holocaust

Neil Tonge

Fellow of the Imperial War Museum, London,
in Holocaust Education

New York

OPELIKA HIGH LIBRARY

Published in 2009 by The Rosen Publishing Group Inc.
29 East 21st Street, New York, NY 10010

Copyright © 2009 Wayland/The Rosen Publishing Group, Inc.

All rights reserved. No part of this book may be reproduced in any
form without permission from the publisher, except by a reviewer.

First Edition

Editor: Camilla Lloyd
Consultants: Dr. R. Gerald Hughes and Dr. James Vaughan
Designer: Phipps Design
Picture researcher: Diana Morris
Maps: Ian Thompson
Indexer and proofreader: Patience Coster

Dedicated to Paul Salmons of the Education Office at the Imperial War Museum

Picture Acknowledgments: The author and publisher would like to thank the
following for allowing their pictures to be reproduced in this publication:
Cover photographs: BL: MEPL/Alamy, BR: Pvt.H.Miller/Corbis; AKG Images: 28, 29,
34; Cody Images: 1, 5, 16, 18, 40, 44; Mary Evans Picture Library: 8, 12, 13, 14, 15,
20, 22, 23, 24, 26, 27, 39, 43; MEPL/Alamy: 1, 9, 40; Courtesy of Harry Goldsmith
(Estate)/USHMM: 47; Imperial War Museum, London: 20, 22, 23, 24, 26, 27, 39;
Courtesy of Ruth Nadelman Lynn/USHMM: 6; Pvt.H.Miller/Corbis: 41; Courtesy of
National Archives & Records Administration, College Park/USHMM: 30; Courtesy of
Fanya Szuster Portnoy/USHMM: 7; Roger-Viollet/Topfoto: 19; Society Of The
Friends Of Music Vienna/Dagli Orti/The Art Archive: 11; Courtesy of Zentrale Stelle
der Landesjustizverwaltungen, Ludwigsberg/USHMM: 32; Courtesy of Eliezer
Zilberis/USHMM: 36.

"The views and opinions expressed in this book and the context in which the images
are used, do not necessarily reflect the views or policy of, nor imply approval or
endorsement by, the United States Holocaust Memorial Museum."

Library of Congress Cataloging-in-Publication Data

Tong, Neil.
 The Holocaust / Neil Tong. -- 1st ed.
    p. cm. -- (Documenting World War II)
 Includes bibliographical references and index.
 ISBN 978-1-4042-1860-4 (lib. bndg.)
 1. Holocaust, Jewish (1939-1945) I. Title.
 D804.3.T66 2008
 940.53'18--dc22
                                    2007042495

Manufactured in China

CONTENTS

CHAPTER 1
BACKGROUND TO THE HOLOCAUST 4

CHAPTER 2
GERMANY AND ANTI-SEMITISM 10

CHAPTER 3
THE NAZIS 16

CHAPTER 4
PERSECUTION OF THE JEWS 22

CHAPTER 5
WAR AND THE HOLOCAUST 32

CHAPTER 6
EXTERMINATION 36

CHAPTER 7
THE DEATH CAMPS 40

CHAPTER 8
THE AFTERMATH 44

TIMELINE 45

GLOSSARY 46

FURTHER INFORMATION AND WEB SITES 47

INDEX 48

OPELIKA HIGH LIBRARY

What is the Holocaust?

During World War II (WWII), Nazi Germany attempted to murder every Jewish person throughout those parts of Europe under German control. The Jews were not the only victims of Nazi brutality. Many other groups of people were forced into slave labor or murdered. "Roma" and "Sinti" people (sometimes called gypsies), Poles, Soviet prisoners of war, people with physical and mental disabilities, "Jehovah's Witnesses," and homosexuals were also killed in vast numbers.

These people were murdered because of Nazi racist beliefs. The German people, or "Aryans," as the Nazis called themselves, thought they were the "master race." All other people, therefore, were inferior, or beneath them and useful only as slaves. Jews, however, were the object of their particular hatred; they were dismissed as not even human but "subhuman."

The term *Holocaust* is used to describe the genocidal plan (*genocide* is the word used to describe the systematic attempt to kill a whole group of people) carried out by the Nazis during WWII to murder all Jewish people. Holocaust is a Greek word, which means "sacrifice to God,"

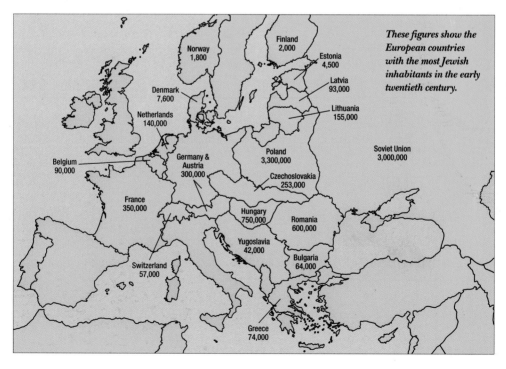

These figures show the European countries with the most Jewish inhabitants in the early twentieth century.

Norway 1,800
Finland 2,000
Estonia 4,500
Latvia 93,000
Denmark 7,600
Lithuania 155,000
Netherlands 140,000
Belgium 90,000
Germany & Austria 300,000
Poland 3,300,000
Soviet Union 3,000,000
Czechoslovakia 253,000
France 350,000
Hungary 750,000
Romania 600,000
Yugoslavia 42,000
Bulgaria 64,000
Switzerland 57,000
Greece 74,000

A selection taking place at the death camp Auschwitz-Birkenau of those who will live to work as slaves and those who will be gassed.

and in the 1950s it came to describe the slaughter of the Jews and other groups of people in WWII. Many Jews use the term *Shoah,* which means "destruction." It means the attempt to destroy all Jews and with them their religion and way of life. Sometimes historians refer to the extermination of Jews in the death camps as the "Final Solution." Adolf Hitler and the other Nazi leaders used the term to mean different things at different stages of their persecution of the Jews.

For example, at one stage it was felt that laws and mass emigration of the Jews might be the "solution," although the term is more usually used by historians to describe the attempt to exterminate all Jewish people in the death camps.

The attacks on Jews were on the widest scale. Six million Jews, including 1,500,000 children, were murdered. One million were shot by execution squads in the Soviet Union and four million were gassed or worked to death in labor camps in the east. By 1942, the killing had become so well organized it was carried out like a factory production line. All the advances in science and technology were used by the Nazis to destroy lives. Jews from all over Europe—men, women, and children—were transported in cattle trucks to the death camps in eastern Europe. When they arrived, usually women with children and the elderly were sent to the gas chambers, and the men and the younger people were kept as slave laborers.

Hatred or dislike of the Jews is known as anti-Semitism and was not just found in Germany. As Nazi conquests spread throughout Europe during WWII, people in other countries actively took part in the killing of Jews, such as the Ukraine.

OPELIKA HIGH LIBRARY

5

The Jews in Europe before the war

Before WWII, Jews all over Europe led very different lives from one another. Some were rich and others were poor. They spoke different languages and believed in different political ideas. Some were doctors and lawyers, others carpenters and factory workers.

Most Eastern European Jews lived in small towns or villages called *shtetls*.

Teichmannbaude T. Rsgb

A group of German Jews on holiday with their friends.

They spoke Yiddish, a language that was a mixture of German and Hebrew, the ancient language of their ancestors. Some lived traditional lives, following the rules laid down in the Bible and in their laws called the *Torah*. They often wore distinctive clothes and formed their own strong communities. Some younger Jews began to leave the *shtetls*, hoping to find a better way of life by working in factories in the towns. Often they were disappointed, finding only low-paid jobs and poverty.

Jewish people in Eastern Europe were often subjected to attacks by non-Jews. Anti-Semitic mobs would destroy Jewish property and sometimes physically harm Jews. These attacks or "pogroms," as they were called, persuaded some Jewish people to leave and seek a life in more tolerant societies. Huge waves of migration began to take place in the late nineteenth and early twentieth centuries to western Europe and the United States.

In an attempt to improve the lives of ordinary working-class Jews in Poland, a socialist movement began called the *Bund*. Jews set up their own social clubs and welfare organizations. They published newspapers, made movies set in the Jewish community, and held concerts of Jewish music. This all helped to maintain a Yiddish culture.

Some Jews, called Zionists, believed that they could only live in a society free of prejudice if they had their own homeland. They chose to go to Palestine, where the ancient Jewish kingdom of Israel had once been. At the end of World War I (WWI), Palestine was given to Britain as a mandate. Britain was allowed to rule the country directly until it was considered ready for independence. Although Britain promised to support the creation of a homeland for the Jews, there was already a large Arab population living in Palestine who resented the arrival of Jewish settlers.

By contrast to the Jews in Eastern Europe, Jews in western Europe tended to be more integrated into society. Although anti-Semitism existed in these countries, Jewish people had the same legal rights as other citizens. Some became traders and bankers, doctors and lawyers, university lecturers and officers in the army, artists and actors. Their contribution to society was sometimes acknowledged, for example, when the German chancellor, Otto von Bismarck, took part in a ceremony at the dedication of a synagogue in Berlin in 1866.

However, occasionally anti-Semitism broke through the surface of society even in western Europe. In 1894, Captain Dreyfus, a Jewish officer in the French army, was accused and put on trial for spying for Germany. On December 22, he was pronounced guilty and sent to the notorious prison on Devil's Island. The evidence against him was flimsy and it later emerged, the anti-Semitic views and attitudes of the military authorities had ensured his conviction. It was not until 1899 that Dreyfus was finally pardoned and his name cleared of the crime.

Many Jews lived in great poverty but often their wealthier Jewish neighbors provided them with food and clothing. This photo was taken in Poland in 1929.

The roots of anti-Semitism

Anti-Semitism has deep historical roots. Over two thousand years ago, the Jews established their own kingdom called Israel in the Middle East but the Romans later conquered it. The Jews rose in revolt against Roman rule. They were no match for the might of Rome, however, and after their rebellion had been crushed and Israel destroyed, many of the Jews fled to other parts of Europe.

In each of the countries throughout the world in which they settled, they were a small minority. In Europe, they formed a separate and different community from the majority of European people, who were Christians.

They were easy targets in times of trouble. Some people argued that the Jews were responsible for the death of Christ and had never accepted the Christian faith. In 1348, when the "Black Death" swept through Europe killing millions of people, some Christians accused them of poisoning the wells and many were burned to death as punishment. Jews were also unpopular because some became money-lenders and charged interest on loans, which was a practice forbidden to Christians.

In 1789, the French Revolution transformed political attitudes. The revolutionaries overthrew the

ENGRAVING

This painting from the fifteenth century shows Strasbourg Jews, including babies, being burned to death unless they agree to convert to the Christian faith.

Source: F.Th. Lix, in *Moderne Kunst*, volume xxii, Plate 3 viii.

monarchy in France and later executed their king and members of the aristocracy. They did so in the name of freedom and equality for all, and this challenged some of the anti-Semitic attitudes. During the following years of the nineteenth century, life improved for Jews throughout western Europe. Governments began to give them equal rights. Yet in many parts of Eastern Europe, where there were large Jewish minorities, anti-Semitism remained strong. Occasionally, and sometimes encouraged by the governments in Poland and the Soviet Union, massacres of and brutality toward Jews broke out.

Just when it seemed as though Jews were becoming more widely accepted into parts of western European society, new anti-Semitic tendencies were emerging based on racism rather than religion. In the mid-1850s, the Frenchman Count Joseph Arthur de Gobineau produced a work entitled *Essay on the Inequality of Human Races,* in which he argued that races had different physical and cultural characteristics. All "high" cultures he described as Aryan, belonging to the Germanic races of Northern Europe. "*Civilisation*" declined, he went on to argue, when Aryans bred with members of "*racially less valuable*" or "*inferior peoples.*" From these racist beliefs a new so-called science called "eugenics" emerged. Believers of eugenics thought that a superior race would emerge if human breeding could be controlled. They set about trying to identify the characteristics that made up these racial differences by measuring skull shapes and sizes, and charting eye and hair color.

SOURCE

BOOK

"*The idea of struggle is as old as life itself, for life is only preserved because of other living things that perish through struggle … In this struggle the stronger, the more able win, while the less able, the weak, lose. Struggle is the father of all things … means of the most bitter struggle.*"

This is the English cover of the translated book that was published in 18-week parts.

Adolf Hitler writing in *Mein Kampf,* published in 1925.

Germany and the Jews

Before 1871, Germany as a single united country had not existed. Instead, German-speaking people lived in a patchwork of separate states. The kingdom of Prussia, which controlled a number of these states in northern Germany, was the largest and most powerful. The German states were all united in 1871 under the Prussian king. The Prussian king became the "kaiser" (emperor) of Germany. This brought into being a superstate and a great industrial nation. Many Germans were proud of what they had achieved and wanted their country to be recognized as a leading nation in the world.

Any group that was not purely German was looked upon with suspicion, and for extreme nationalists, the Jews represented just such a group. The superiority of the German people, or *volk*, was seen as arising from a sense of community based on ancient blood ties. They saw the *volk* as having special characteristics, preserving the warrior virtues of duty, honor, courage, and loyalty.

Influenced by the racist writings of the time, extremely anti-Semitic nationalist views became more commonly held. In 1881, Eugene Duhring, an economist, argued that the feelings, thinking, and behavior of humans were racially determined. The "*scarcely human*" Jews, he argued, were the enemies of all nations and particularly the Germans.

Anti-Semitism was present in all aspects of German life. Richard Wagner, the famous German composer, frequently accused Jews, particularly Jewish musicians, of being a harmful alien element in German culture. He argued that Jewish musicians were only capable of producing music that was shallow because they had no connection with the genuine spirit of the German people, "*…with all our speaking and writing in favor of the Jew's emancipation (equal rights with Germans), we always felt instinctively repelled by actual contact with them.*" In the conclusion to his writings, he wrote that they must "*go under.*" Although this has been taken to mean their extermination, some historians have argued that he only meant that Judaism should disappear and Jews should become fully integrated into German society.

Despite his hatred of Judaism, Wagner had several Jewish friends. One of his best friends was Hermann Levi, a practicing Jew and the son of a rabbi. He freely praised Hermann's talent and even requested him to be one of his pallbearers at his funeral.

This is a painting of the German composer Richard Wagner. Adolf Hitler was a fanatical admirer of Wagner's beliefs and his music. He held many of Wagner's original scores in his Berlin underground headquarters.

Wagner's views on race would probably be considered unimportant were it not for the influence of his son-in-law, Houston Stewart Chamberlain. In 1899, his book *The Foundations of the Nineteenth Century,* was published and it became an immediate bestseller in many countries in western Europe. The book was a racist work, promoting the idea of an Aryan "super-race." This book was very important in the development of Hitler's racial beliefs. It greatly influenced his ideas and those of his fellow Nazis.

11

Hitler and anti-Semitism

Adolf Hitler was born in Austria in 1889 and grew up in an anti-Semitic society. He said he first became anti-Semitic when he wandered the streets of Vienna after failing to get into art school before WWI. Vienna at that time contained a large number of Jews, and many pamphlets and articles expressing anti-Semitic hatred were circulating.

In 1914, Hitler volunteered for war service in the German army. At that time, Austria was the leading nation in the vast multinational Austro-Hungarian Empire. Hitler joined the German army in the belief that Germany more truly represented the purity of the Aryan race, rather than the mixture of countries that made up the Austro-Hungarian Empire.

During the war, he fought bravely and rose to the rank of corporal, winning the Iron Cross twice, 1st and 2nd class, a high military distinction. In November 1918, while he was recovering in a hospital from a gas attack injury, he heard of Germany's armistice and surrender to the Allies. Meanwhile, in Germany, the kaiser had abdicated and a new republican government had come to power. It met at Weimar, a small German town, because it was felt that Berlin, the capital city, was too dangerous. Hitler, like many of his fellow soldiers, became convinced that the Weimar

Nazis march into Munich following the Hitler Putsch in November 1923.

Government, which contained some Jews, had "*stabbed the army in the back*" by surrendering. There were more non-Jewish members of the new republican government than Jews, but this did not stop Hitler from making his accusation. From then on, according to his beliefs, the Jews were the sinister force that was destroying Germany.

When he was released from the hospital, he returned to Munich and was employed by the army as a political lecturer, reporting on the activities of the various nationalist parties that were springing up. However, when he attended a meeting of one tiny party, the German Workers' Party, his life changed forever.

In 1919, Hitler joined the German Workers' Party. Within two years he had become the leader, or *Fuhrer,* of the renamed National Socialist German Workers' Party, or Nazi Party. In 1923, he felt his party was strong enough to overthrow the government of Bavaria. The attempt was called the "Hitler Putsch" or the "Munich Putsch." The attempt failed, and Hitler was tried and sentenced to five years in prison, but only had to serve nine months. While he was in prison, in comfortable surroundings, he set down his ideas and plans. In 1925, the first volume of his book, *Mein Kampf,* translated as "My Struggle" or "My Battle" was published. The book applied Social Darwinism, nationalism, and racism to post-WWI Germany.

SOURCE

BOOK

"*If just once at the beginning or course of the war, we had exposed 12,000 or 15,000 of these Hebrew [Jewish] corrupters of the people to the poison gas that hundreds of our best German workers of every extraction and every profession had to endure at the front, the sacrifice of millions of men would not have been in vain.*"

Hitler's reaction to Germany's surrender at the end of WWI. An extract from *Mein Kampf,* 1925.

By 1939, 5.2 million copies of **Mein Kampf** *had been sold.*

The growth of anti-Semitism in Germany 1918–33

One of the reasons for Hitler's rise to power was that many Germans were sympathetic to his views. A distinct group of people like the Jews provided a convenient scapegoat upon whom the Germans could focus their resentment. This resentment had been caused mainly by the economic situation after WWI. The Nazis exploited this in two ways. On one hand, some Jews had become wealthy bankers, like the Rothschilds. According to the Nazis, these Jews were making fortunes while the workers were receiving pitiful wages.

On the other hand, some Jews had been leading members of the Communist Party (the Bolsheviks) in the Soviet Union. According to the Nazis, they had overthrown the bankers and the rich in their own country and wanted other countries throughout the world to follow their example. To German nationalists, German communists, with Jewish leaders like Rosa Luxemburg and Karl Leibknecht, could destroy their country.

The Nazis linked the two ideas together. In their view, this was evidence of a world conspiracy by Jewish bankers on one hand, and Jewish communists on the other hand, to take over the world.

These prejudices fell on fertile ground. The army, civil service, churches, and the law showed strong elements of anti-Semitism. In 1921, a document called *The Protocols of the Elders of Zion* was

Source: Cover of *The Protocols of the Elders of Zion*.

published in which Jews stated how they were planning to take over the world. Even when it was proved to be a Russian forgery dating back to the 1890s, many anti-Semites continued to believe it was true. The document was used as evidence that Jewish leaders were formulating secret plans to take over the world.

The real impact of the Jews on German society was debatable. Jews made up less than 1 percent of the total population. They positively contributed to society. Half of the Nobel Prizes for contributions to the arts and to science were awarded to them. During WWI, 95,000 Jewish soldiers had served in the army; 35,000 were awarded medals and 12,000 had died for their country. Despite this, many were prepared to believe that the

Jews had caused their problems.

The Nazi Party was deeply anti-Semitic, but before 1928, it had made little progress in winning elections. In some areas of Germany, the anti-Semitic messages were well received, but in others they had little effect. The party learned to take advantage of anti-Semitism in areas where it existed and to play it down where it did not. Despite their clever tactics, the Nazis only succeeded in persuading 3 percent of the population to vote for them.

By 1932, however, there had been a dramatic change in the fortunes of the Nazi Party. The collapse of the German economy in a worldwide depression sparked off by the collapse of the U.S. stock market made almost six million Germans unemployed. The Nazis blamed the Weimar Government and democracy for failing Germany. The Nazis promised, through their strong leadership, that they would solve the economic problems and get Germans back to work again. They were widely believed, and by 1932 were the largest party.

ILLUSTRATION

The picture below shows the Nazi racial stereotype of the handsome, healthy Aryan German worker versus the anti-Semitic image of the fat, greedy, middle-aged Jew.

Source: Unattributed illustration from the book *Trust No Fox on the Heath and No Jew on his Word*, Stürmer Press, Germany, 1935.

The Nazis come to power

In late 1932, the economic depression eased and Nazi votes dipped. Although Hitler had emerged as the leader of the largest single party in the *Reichstag*, he had only won 33 percent of the vote. The other political parties in the *Reichstag* could still out-vote him if they joined forces with one another. President Hindenburg, who had the power to appoint the chancellor to form a new government, did not want Hitler, because he regarded him as a dangerous figure. After some indecision, the near-senile, 85-year-old Hindenburg was finally persuaded by his own son and conservative nationalists, such as Franz von Papen, to give the post to Hitler.

The Nazis were overjoyed. They had feared that power might slip from their fingers, but instead their leader had been appointed to the most powerful political position in Germany. Hitler had no intention of sharing this position. The outbreak of a fire in the *Reichstag* gave him his chance to consolidate power. No one knows

Heinrich Himmler became an important figure in Nazi Germany. He was determined that the SS (Nazi eltite) should become a ruling class based on racial grounds. All recruits had to pass a rigorous racial test. Only perfect Aryans—tall, blond-haired, and blue-eyed candidates—were accepted.

precisely how the fire began, but a Dutch communist, Van der Lubbe, was discovered inside the building. The Nazis used the arrest of Van der Lubbe as an excuse to round up and imprison communist leaders, claiming that they had uncovered a plot to seize the government.

Within 18 months of being appointed Chancellor, Hitler had turned himself into a dictator. How was he able to achieve this legally? In order to change the "Constitution" (rules of government), he needed a two-thirds majority. Firstly, he banned the Communist Party because of its so-called involvement in the *Reichstag* Fire and they were not allowed to take their seats in the parliament. Then he bullied and persuaded the other *Reichstag* members. On March 23, 1933, he forced through the "Enabling Act," which meant he could make laws without consulting the members of the *Reichstag* or the president. When Hindenburg died a few months later, he combined the posts of chancellor and president. Hitler's hold over Germany was complete.

By 1934, there was only one legal party allowed and Hitler was the undisputed leader of that party. A new, powerful party organization called the SS ensured that all opposition was crushed. The SS (*Schutzstaffel*) formed in 1925, was a relatively small section of the Party until Heinrich Himmler became its leader in 1929. The SS

SOURCE

SPEECH

"The first principle and recognition for us was and is the recognition of the values of blood and selection … the nature of the physical selection process was to concentrate on the choice of those who came physically closest to the ideal of the Nordic man. External features such as size and a racially appropriate appearance played and still play a role here.

"I know there are some in Germany who feel sick at the sight of this black uniform (worn by the SS); we can understand their feelings and do not expect many people to love us. All those who have Germany's interests at heart will and should respect us and those who have guilty consciences toward the Fuhrer or the nation should fear us … we shall ensure that never again will the Jewish-Bolshevist [communist] revolution of subhumanity be unleashed in Germany, the heart of Europe."

Source: Heinrich Himmler explains the purpose of the SS in a speech in 1935.

attracted some of the most fanatical and well-educated idealists who were the elite of the Nazi Party. By 1936, all police powers were under Himmler's control, and the SS became the most powerful force in the state.

Nazi propaganda

It was not only through the use of terror that the Nazi Party stayed in power. From 1933 onward, the Nazis used all the communication channels available to them in an attempt to win over the hearts and minds of the German people. Hitler entrusted this task to Josef Goebbels, who became "Minister of Popular Enlightenment and Propaganda." Goebbels brought all radio stations under his control and censored the press, movies, theater, literature, and art.

Movies were very popular at this time. Goebbels used them to spread Nazi propaganda. Anti-Semitic pictures included *Jude Suss*, which told the story of an evil Jew who tried to take control of a German state in the eighteenth century. The most hate-filled movie was called *The Eternal Jew*, a documentary illustrating the disease and corruption that Nazis claimed had been spread by Jews throughout history.

Art and culture were strictly controlled. Goebbels set up a "Reich Chamber of Culture." All musicians, writers, and actors had to be members and if they were thought unsuitable, they would not be able to find work. Goebbels also banned books written by Jews or enemies of the Nazis.

Josef Goebbels (right) was the son of an office worker. He had been unable to serve in the German army during WWI because of a crippled foot. He joined the party in 1922 and was put in charge of propaganda.

Germans were expected to belong to one of the many Nazi-controlled organizations. By 1939, the "Hitler Youth" movement had almost nine million members. The aim of the Hitler Youth was to ensure that young people remained loyal to the

published depicting caricatures of Jews as evil, scheming people.

It is difficult to tell how successful the Nazi propaganda was. The Nazis set up their own organizations to test

SOURCE

POSTER

Audiences were only admitted at the beginning of the movie and had to see the entire program. This meant that the Nazi propaganda documentaries shown before the main feature were seen.

A poster for the film *The Eternal Jew*, 1940.

Fatherland (Germany) and to Hitler. There were Nazi organizations for young girls and for workers in factories. Street wardens were appointed to report disloyalty, and even children were encouraged to inform the Party if they heard any remarks against the Nazis.

Education was thought to be the key to making "good" German citizens. Jewish teachers were dismissed immediately, as were any others who were suspected of being opposed to the Nazis. Lessons in race were made compulsory. Children's books were

public opinion. The evidence from the surveys suggests that the Party remained popular and Hitler more popular than the Party itself. This was probably because the Nazi Party reduced unemployment and began to make Germany a power in the world once more. Older people, however, tended to be more mistrustful, whereas the younger generation was more easily swayed by Nazi propaganda.

The Nazi racial state

Hitler claimed that the central factor in world history was racial struggle. In comparison to the Aryan race, all others, he believed, were inferior, or in the case of the Jews, actually subhuman. He held that the Germanic Aryan *volk* must remain racially superior by not marrying into other races. In order to create the necessary space for the expanding master race, German forces would have to fight for *lebensraum,* or "living space," in Eastern Europe, and those inferior races they conquered would be killed or enslaved to work for them.

Since their aim was to achieve the purity of the German race, the Nazis decided to weed out those that they considered "not worthy of life"—the physically and mentally disabled. One of the first acts of the Nazi regime was a law allowing the compulsory sterilization of those with hereditary illnesses to prevent disease being passed on. Over the next 12 years, about 350,000 people were sterilized. By 1939, the policy of sterilization had developed into an extermination policy. A special unit, T4, was

SOURCE

MEDICAL REGISTER

This photo shows a page from the medical register of a sanatorium where handicapped and insane people were murdered. The page gives names, ages, nationalities, and "official" causes of death.

Source: From Hadamar "sanatorium" in Austria, April 1945.

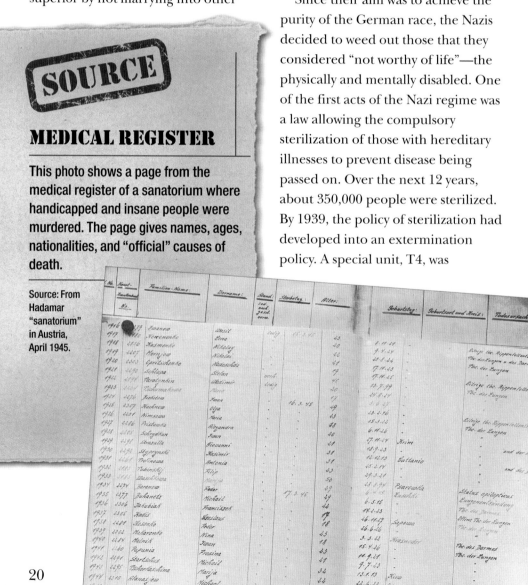

established to kill disabled children. They were killed by starvation, lethal injection, or by gas in mobile vans or shower gas chambers. Adults were included next. By 1944, 200,000 people had been murdered in this way. The techniques of the euthanasia, or "mercy killing," program were later used in the Holocaust.

In contrast, the Nazis did much to encourage healthy Germans to have children. Mothers with large families were given awards like the Mother's Cross; gold for having eight children, silver for six, and bronze for four.

After 1933, doctors and scientists offered courses on "eugenics and race" to nurses, teachers, and civil servants so that they could identify the groups seen as a danger to Nazi society. These included homosexuals, beggars, alcoholics, and criminals. Many of these people were sent to concentration camps. The 30,000 gypsies in Germany were also targeted. The gypsies consisted of two groups— Roma, who continued to travel, and Sinti, who had set up permanent homes. It was difficult to define who a gypsy was, so in 1936, Dr. Robert Ritter set up a research unit in an attempt to classify them. By the late 1930s, many had been rounded up and placed in special camps. Some ended up in Auschwitz concentration camp.

Jews, however, remained Hitler's prime target. The future of Germany's 500,000 Jews was under great threat.

RECOLLECTION

"My mother said, 'Come on, my boy, it's time to go to hospital.' The doctor was wearing an SA uniform. He made two cuts around my testicles. Sometimes I'm glad I can't have children. At least they were spared the shame I lived with."

The SA were Nazi stormtroopers. They acted like a Nazi paramilitary unit.

Source: Thomas Holzhauser, a black victim of the Nazis' forced sterilization program.

PROPAGANDA FILM

"Sterilization is a simple surgical operation. In the last 70 years, our people have increased by 50% while in the same period the number of hereditary ill have risen by 450%. If this were to continue, there would be one hereditarily ill person to four people. An endless column of horror would march into the nation."

Source: From the commentary for the 1937 film *Victims of the Past* ordered by Hitler to be shown in all 5,300 German theaters before *I Accuse*, the main feature, which approved euthanasia, was shown.

The persecution begins

Anti-Semitism was a driving force behind the Nazi Party's beliefs, but these beliefs had then to be translated into practical policies.

In 1933, there were 503,000 Jews in Germany, making up just under 1 percent of the population. Most of this number lived in cities and many led prosperous lives as lawyers, teachers, and doctors. Hitler was afraid that if he moved too quickly against the Jews, it might harm the economic stability of the country and upset international opinion, which could lead to a boycott of German goods.

In early 1933, Jewish property was destroyed and synagogues attacked by the Nazi's SA (*Sturm-Abteilung*, meaning "stormtroopers"). When these actions provoked international protests against the treatment of German Jews, Hitler tried to explain

A member of the SA gives the Nazi salute and bars the entrance to a Jewish shop in April 1933. The shop windows have notices posted on them saying "Germans! Watch out! Don't buy from Jews!"

they were simply the result of the popular anger of the people. To punish Germany, the U.S. called for an international boycott of German goods. Outraged, Hitler accused the American Jews of being behind this and in revenge called for Germans to stop dealing with Jewish businesses. On April 1, 1933, SA thugs stood outside Jewish shops and businesses and ordered fellow Germans not to deal with them. Passersby remained unconvinced and after one day the boycott of Jewish businesses collapsed.

Hitler decided to increase the pressure and the persecution of Jews legally, instead of leaving it to the SA. From April 1933 onward, there was a flood of anti-Semitic laws. The most important of these was the "Law of the Restoration of the Professional Civil Service," which meant that Jews were thrown out of all government posts. Other anti-Semitic measures followed and were introduced in many areas of daily life. The number of Jews attending state schools was reduced through a law supposedly aimed at reducing overcrowding.

Jewish people found life increasingly difficult in Germany. As well as facing new anti-Semitic laws,

they also had to endure daily attacks in the press, especially in Julius Streicher's *Der Stürmer* newspaper. From 1933 onward, it was regarded as the Nazi official newspaper and it

SOURCE

ILLUSTRATION

People were encouraged to believe that Jews were evil. In this cartoon, a Jewish doctor invites an Aryan into his consulting room. The caption reads: "behind the glasses twinkle the eyes of a criminal and round the blubbery lips plays a grin."

Source: This example is taken from *The Poison Mushroom: A Stürmer book for Young and Old*, 1938.

poured out the most sustained attacks on Jews. Germans were discouraged from having any contacts with Jews. Teachers humiliated Jewish children at school. Jewish university students were driven out. They were banned from all clubs and organizations. They were pressured to sell their businesses at a fraction of their worth to non-Jews.

Few Germans spoke out against such measures. Although some approved of them, others were undoubtedly scared into silence.

Escape from Germany

During 1934, the government suspended the attacks on Jews. Jewish businesses were playing too important a role in Germany's economic recovery to be disrupted. Nazis still vented their feelings, however, and Jews were insulted in the street and beaten up.

*A banner that reads "**Jews are not wanted here**" hangs over the entrance to the village of Rosenheim in Bavaria.*

On their own initiative, some villages and towns put up signs saying "Jews not wanted here" or "Jew-free resort." Some hotels and restaurants refused to serve Jews.

Some German Jews tried to emigrate but often found their way barred. They were not allowed to take their money out of Germany, and some countries

were reluctant to admit too many of them because they feared greater unemployment or criticism from their own electorate.

Despite the difficulties, 37,000 Jews left Germany in 1933. They included some famous people, such as the scientist, Albert Einstein. In 1934, when attacks were less frequent, Jewish emigration fell to 23,000. Older Jews were often reluctant to leave. They had lived all their lives in Germany and thought of themselves as Germans. Many believed that things would settle down when the Nazis had been in power for a few years.

However, things got worse for the Jewish population. The Nazis wanted the Jews to leave the country. Rich Jews were permitted to take their wealth to Palestine (see page 6).

Britain had promised to help create a homeland in Palestine for the Jews, but was only allowing a limited number to enter. If too many Jews were admitted to Palestine, it would anger the Arab population and Britain would find herself stuck between two hostile communities.

In July 1938, delegates from 32 nations met at Evian Les-Bains in France to try to find an international solution to the increasing problem of the influx of refugees from Germany and the newly-annexed Austria. Nearly all of the countries put forward a range of objections to taking the refugees.

Germany's annexation with Austria

SOURCE

RECOLLECTION

The British government agreed to take some Jewish children. It would accept Jewish and non-Aryan children up to the age of 17, but their sponsors had to provide a bond of £50 (about $2,000 in today's money) so that the children would not be supported out of taxes. The intention was to give the children an education and then return them home when that was possible. Almost 10,000 children were evacuated from Germany and Austria between December 1938 and the end of August 1939. Many never saw their parents again.

"It was obvious that I was not welcome. The father had agreed to pay for me to come to England as his patriotic duty. His wife did not like the idea of a foreign stranger in her house. I could speak no English. If it had not been for their daughters and their maid, I would have been desperately unhappy. I never saw my parents again. They were elderly and sent to Auschwitz where they were killed."

Edith Weiss: A Kindertransport child.

in 1938 (called the *Anschluss*) was Hitler's first major move to create an empire. Most Austrian Jews chose to emigrate if they could.

The Nuremberg Laws 1935

In the spring of 1935, there was pressure within the Nazi leadership to take more effective action to restrict Jewish life. Nazi newspapers published stories alleging that Jews had raped thousands of German girls. At a local level, Nazis stepped up their campaign against Jewish businesses.

In August 1935, 16,000 people bought tickets for a Nazi rally in Berlin to hear Julius Streicher speak. Streicher was a fanatical anti-Semite.

Following these lurid accounts in the newspapers, demands began to grow for a "blood protection law" to prevent marriages between Jews and Germans. In July 1935, registrars were ordered to stop performing mixed marriage ceremonies.

Hitler used the massive party rally at Nuremberg in September 1935, to announce sweeping measures against

the Jews. Introducing the new laws, Hitler declared that he hoped they would provide a future basis for German-Jewish relations, but if they failed then he would have to seek a Final Solution. The Nuremberg Laws were as follows:

The Law for the Protection of German Blood and German Honor forbade marriage and sexual relations between Jews and Germans. No Jew was allowed to employ a domestic servant under the age of 45. Jews were not permitted to display the national flag.

The Reich Citizenship Law stripped Jews of their German citizenship. Jews were now regarded as aliens with no rights and very little protection from the law.

The Law for the Protection of the Genetic Health of the German People insisted that a medical certificate was needed before marriage. This was not just to ensure that couples were fit and healthy, but to verify that they had also been "racially tested" to make sure they were Aryan.

However, finding a legal definition of who was a Jew was difficult. Some thought that having one Jewish parent was enough to classify Jews, others said it had to be both sets of grandparents. Legal and racial experts attempted to agree on a definition. In November 1935, the **First Supplementary Decree** on the **Reich Citizenship Law** was issued. A "full" Jew was someone who had three Jewish grandparents, or someone who had two Jewish grandparents and was married to a Jew. Those who had fewer Jewish relatives were defined as *Mischlinge* (half-breeds). If someone had only one Jewish grandparent then they were generally regarded as an Aryan unless they belonged to the Jewish religious community or had married a Jew.

The Nuremberg Laws were difficult to put into practice. The Nazis prided themselves on the fact that they could define someone's race scientifically, but it was a very difficult job and relied on parentage or religious practice for a working definition.

SOURCE

PROPAGANDA

The photo below is a typical Nazi propaganda image of an Aryan youth with a Swastika flag proclaiming the bright future of Germany.

Source: Nazi propaganda image, 1933.

The calm before the storm

In 1936, Germany staged the Olympic Games. Anxious to make the games a success and concerned that some countries might withdraw their teams because of Germany's anti-Semitic laws, Hitler played down the Nazi campaigns against the Jews. Hitler saw the Olympics as an opportunity to display the physical superiority of Germans as the master race. The Olympics held in Berlin were a great propaganda success for the Nazis, and Germany finished at the top of the league table for medals. Once the Olympics had been staged, fanatics within the Nazi Party called for campaigns for greater measures against the Jews. At a 1936 party conference, Julius Streicher, the most fanatical anti-Semite, claimed that the Nazis, "*had declared war on the Jews which [would] end in their annihilation.*" By the end of 1937, Germany was re-arming and was less afraid of international opinion and pressure.

Hermann Goering was in charge of the economy. His aim was to secretly prepare Germany for war. He sought greater control over Jewish businesses, putting pressure on them to sell at very low prices to Aryan managers. This process was aided by the **Decree for the Registration of Jewish Property** (April 1938). This prepared the way for the

The Brandenburg Gate was decorated with swastikas for the Olympic Games in Berlin in August 1936.

confiscation of Jewish property. Over the following 12 months, only 20 percent of Jewish businesses avoided being taken over by Aryans. In the same year, male Jews were forced to add "Israel" and female Jews "Sarah" to their existing names for ease of identification.

A hardening of Nazi attitudes took place when Germany took over Austria (known as the *Anschluss*) in March 1938. Most of the Austrians welcomed the uniting of the countries, despite the fact that the Treaty of Versailles signed at the end of WWI had forbidden it. *Anschluss* was accompanied by spontaneous attacks on Jews by Austrians. Jews were beaten up and forced to wash the sidewalks; others had their homes and businesses broken into and looted. By the end of the year, most Austrian businesses were in the hands of Aryans.

The SS was increasing its influence in anti-Semitic affairs. The SS established a section of their organization, which collected and collated information on Jewish individuals and organizations. The deputy head of this organization was Adolf Eichmann, an Austrian Nazi. Adolf Eichmann built up a reputation as an expert on "Jewish matters."

Adolf Eichmann returned to Austria and began measures to speed up the emigration of Jews. Jews could hand over their business and get a visa to leave the country in one day, but they

BOOK COVER

Jazz and the saxophone were banned as symbols of an "inferior black" culture. This image below was the cover of a catalogue for an exhibition of art in 1938 that the Nazis condemned.

had to leave with practically nothing. By November 1938, he had arranged the emigration of 50,000 Jews. He was later brought to trial in Israel in 1961 and was subsequently hung for war crimes and crimes against humanity in the following year.

The November Pogroms—
Kristallnacht

By 1938, Hitler had removed the more conservative forces of his government and opened the way for more bitter, direct attacks on the Jews. An opportunity for one such attack came in November 1938. On November 7, a 17-year-old Polish Jew shot and killed a German embassy official in Paris. He had committed the crime out of revenge for the mistreatment of his parents and other Polish Jews in Germany, who had been taken from their homes and dumped on the border with Poland.

Using the murder as a pretext, Goebbels launched a national campaign against the Jews. On November 8–9, Jewish businesses, homes, and synagogues were attacked by Nazi mobs. The violence of the following night (*Kristallnacht,* or the

> *"Of course, it was a terrible night. If Jews were caught out on the streets, they were beaten. My father ventured out the next morning for tobacco. A mob surrounded him and attacked him."*
>
> Edith Weiss remembering *Kristallnacht* in Vienna, Austria, in 1938.

"Night of Broken Glass") was even more ferocious. Over 8,000 Jewish businesses were destroyed, 200 synagogues burned, hundreds of Jews beaten up, and 100 murdered. The police and the fire department were instructed not to intervene unless Aryan property was threatened. During the next few days, over 30,000 Jewish men were taken to concentration camps. Most were released but only on the condition that they emigrated.

The Nazi leadership was surprised by the level of violence. Himmler was critical of the chaotic nature of the SA's attacks. Goering (a leading member of the Nazi party and commander of the *Luftwaffe*, the German Air Force) was concerned about the destruction of property. Indeed, the action proved to be unpopular with many ordinary Germans, too. Foreign newspapers were quick to see that *Kristallnacht* had not been a spontaneous wave of violence but an organized attack coordinated by the German government. Little protest was heard from within Germany, however, since it was becoming increasingly dangerous for people to openly oppose Nazi policies.

From this moment on, the Nazis became more determined to organize and plan the campaign against the Jews. On November 12, Goering held a meeting with officials to plan their reaction to the *Kristallnacht*. As a result of the meeting, the Jews were blamed

SOURCE

SPEECH

"In the course of my life, I have often been a prophet and have usually been ridiculed for it. During the time of my struggle for power, it was in the first instance only the Jewish race that received my prophecies with laughter when I said I would one day take over the leadership of the state ... Today I will once more be a prophet: if the international Jewish financiers in and outside of Europe should succeed in plunging Europe once more into a world war, then the result will not be the bolshevizing [making communist] of the Earth and thus the victory of Jewry, but of the annihilation of the Jewish race in Europe."

Hitler in a speech to the *Reichstag* in January 1939.

for the destruction and the government seized the victims' insurance money. The victims were also required to pay a collective fine of 1,000 million marks as compensation for the murder of the German diplomat Ernst von Rath in Paris. Jews were now totally excluded from economic and social life. They were excluded from businesses and places of entertainment. The outbreak of war further increased their persecution.

War and conquest

On September 1, 1939, Germany invaded Poland. Britain and France demanded that Germany withdraw her armies otherwise they would declare war. In a secret deal with Germany, the Soviet Union invaded from the east and Poland was carved up between the two powers. Britain and France did little but mobilize their troops and man France's border with Germany. In the following year, German forces smashed through the Netherlands and Belgium, and overran France in less than six weeks. The German occupation of Yugoslavia and Greece followed. Norway and Denmark had already been occupied. Britain, although weakened, stood alone against Nazi Germany.

Hitler's conquests in Europe proved to be the turning point in the persecution of the Jews. Millions of Jews in Europe were now under Nazi rule. At this point, it appeared that Hitler had no immediate plans to "solve" the Jewish question or extend the persecution.

The forced emigration of Jews was still favored by Nazi leaders. In 1940, Reinhard Heydrich, the deputy leader of the SS, asked the German Foreign Ministry to select a place for the Jews' resettlement. The ministry suggested Madagascar, an island off the southeast coast of Africa. Initially, this solution was greeted with enthusiasm; at that time, Madagascar was a colony governed by German-occupied France. However, Britain still controlled the sea lanes, and for this reason the plan proved impossible to carry out.

These women and children from Dvinsk in Latvia were later shot by the Einsatzgruppen—*a Nazi police force.*

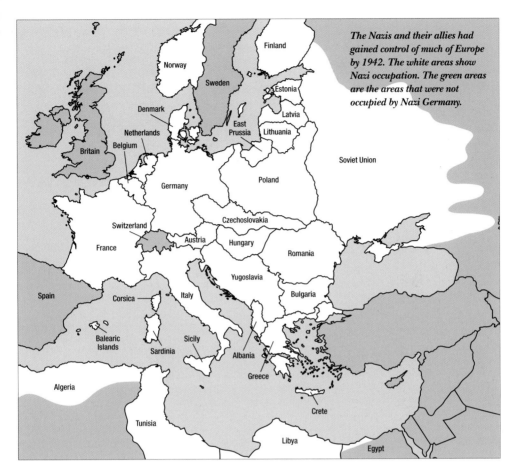

The Nazis and their allies had gained control of much of Europe by 1942. The white areas show Nazi occupation. The green areas are the areas that were not occupied by Nazi Germany.

The conquest of Poland showed the Nazi's murderous intentions. In August 1939, a special police force unit—the *Einsatzgruppen*—was formed. Their orders were to "render harmless" the professional class of Poland. This instruction meant to murder the leading members of Polish society. Thousands of Poles were shot. This was the beginning of Hitler's plan for *lebensraum* in the east.

Germany absorbed much of the Polish territory into the Third Reich (Nazi Germany) and the Soviet Union did the same with its share.

The Nazis left a central area of Poland, the "General Government," free as an area to concentrate Poles, Jews, gypsies, and others they did not want in the *Reich*.

The Jews were terrorized. Although they had not been given official orders to murder Jews, the *Einsatzgruppen* and the SS carried out mass shootings. All Jews were forced to wear a white armband with the "Star of David" for identification. Jewish males were subjected to two years forced labor. The forced deportation caused chaos and had to be halted temporarily.

The ghettos

Shortly after the conquest of Poland, the Nazis began to order all Jews to live in certain parts of Polish cities. This was to ensure that when the time came in 1940 for them to be deported farther east, the move could be easily managed.

Most Polish cities already had Jewish districts. Jews outside of these areas were now forced to move into them. Jews in the countryside were also ordered to move into those areas. The city of Lodz was the site of the first sealed ghetto from which Jews were not allowed to leave.

Jews in the ghettos were instructed to organize their own councils (*Judenraat*) to keep "an orderly community life." They had to provide

Rations in the Warsaw ghetto were cut to a minimum. Children became the first victims of starvation.

lists of names of all the people inside the ghettos and to organize labor groups to work for the Germans. In Lodz, Chaim Rumkovski became a virtual dictator over the 150,000 Jews living there. He issued money bearing his signature and stamps that bore his face.

The ghetto in Warsaw, the capital of Poland, was the largest. The "Jewish Council" was ordered to build a wall around the ghetto at its own expense. More and more Jews were crowded into this tiny area, some 500,000 in 62,000 sq miles (100,000 per sq km). Only those Jews who were working were given rations. In a short time, death from starvation and disease began to wipe out the population.

By 1943, most of Warsaw's Jews had been deported to the east and only 60,000 were left in the ghetto. When German troops moved into the ghetto to round up all the remaining Jews, they were met with a volley of fire from handguns and rifles and were pelted with gasoline bombs. With only one rifle between 150 men, the Jews knew what the outcome would be, yet they preferred to die fighting. They managed to hold out for a month against the German army. Some tried to escape through the sewers. By the end of the Warsaw Uprising, 56,000 Jews had been killed or sent to the death camps. The untrained Jewish fighters fought courageously, but only 16 German soldiers were killed.

SPEECH

"*The creation of the ghetto is, of course, only a provisional measure. I reserve for myself the decision as to the point in time and the means by which the ghetto … will be cleared of Jews. The final goal, at any rate, must be to lance the festering boil.*"

A speech by Freiderich Ubelhor, German administrator of Lodz, April 1940.

DIARY

"*On the streets children are crying in vain, children who are dying of hunger. They howl, beg, sing, moan, shiver with cold, without underwear, without clothing, without shoes, in rags, sack, flannel, which are bound in strips round the emaciated skeletons, children swollen with hunger … typhus, dysentery, tuberculosis … The hospitals are so terribly overcrowded that there are 2–3 patients in every bed. Those who do not lie in a bed find a place on the floor in rooms and corridors.*"

From the diary of Stanislav Rozycki, a visitor to the Warsaw ghetto.

A war of extermination

On June 22, 1941, Hitler ordered the launch of "Operation Barbarossa," the invasion of the Soviet Union. This was the war he had always wanted—a racial war to kill or enslave the Soviet people and create *lebensraum* for the German people. The success of the German army, at first, was amazing. Within weeks, three million Soviet soldiers had fallen into German hands and huge areas of the Soviet Union had been overrun. Jews and communist party officials were usually immediately shot. Those Jews not killed were packed into ghettos as they had been in Poland. Although some German generals had protested against the widespread shootings in Poland, they did not do so in the Soviet Union. Some of the leaders of the Soviet communist government were Jewish, and the Nazis believed that communism was a Jewish plot to take over the world. Therefore, when Jews were murdered in the Soviet Union, Nazis believed communism was also being destroyed.

Einsatzgruppen led by SS officers carried out the work of mass shootings of men, women, and children in the conquered areas of the Soviet Union. There were four *Einsatzgruppen* formations, A to D, who carried out the shootings. They were each about 1,000 strong and were divided into smaller units called *Einsatzcommandos*.

Although hundreds of thousands of people were murdered by these execution squads, the Nazis had not taken the final step toward the extermination of all Jews in Europe. Up until mid-August 1941, it was assumed that 30 million Soviets, including Jews, would be resettled in

With few weapons and no training, Jews formed their own resistance groups.

Siberia and that the freed land would be given to 4.5 million German settlers.

By September 1941, however, the mass murder of thousands of Soviet Jews, including women and children, was well underway. Now hundreds of victims were lined up alongside huge trenches, told to undress as a further humiliation, and then shot into the trenches.

Murder on this scale was problematic. For a start, large trenches had to be dug in which to bury the bodies. It was difficult sometimes to control the victims, who would panic, cry out, and fight back. Many of those shot were only wounded. Some of the executioners complained that it was too "unpleasant" a task for the police units to carry out, and it was felt that a more scientific solution needed to be found.

Jewish resistance to Nazi persecution took many forms. Many Jews resisted by keeping their religion alive, their families together, their schools open, and by recording details of the persecution and massacres they had experienced at the hands of the Nazis. When resistance groups were able to form, Nazi reactions were ferocious with many Jews dying in Nazi reprisals. The odds were overwhelmingly bad for the Jewish resistance fighters. In Poland, there were at least 28 groups of Jewish resistance fighters. There were also armed uprisings in five of the concentration camps.

RECOLLECTION

"Struggling to stay alive for another day was a form of resistance. Escaping from the ghetto or hiding in a bunker was resistance. Resistance was giving birth to a child in the ghetto, sharing food with others, praying in a congregation, singing in a chorus, studying the Bible, planting flowers in the ghetto, keeping a diary under the shadow of death."

The words of a young resistance fighter, Chaim Lazar.

RECOLLECTION

"When we attacked we would move like lightning, and I used to shoot Germans on the left and on the right. Sometimes I threw grenades at them. The best thing was dynamite, though with dynamite we always worked at night. We used to creep on all fours to the railroad tracks, attach the wires, and hide them. Then we hid ... and waited for the train whistle. Sometimes they let me light the fuse. You had to time it just right, so that the whole train would go boom!"

Another unnamed resistance fighter from a ghetto.

The Final Solution

In July 1941, with German conquests at their peak, Hitler called upon the SS to develop a plan to kill all Europe's Jews, not just those in the Soviet Union. Operation Barbarossa had come across problems. Despite the early successes

SOURCE

SPEECH

"... the soldier is not simply a fighter according to the rules of war, but the supporter of a ruthless racial ideology and the avenger of all the bestialities which have been inflicted on the German nation ... for this reason, the soldiers must show full understanding for the necessity of severe atonement required of the Jewish subhumans."

German Field Marshal, von Reichenau, in a speech in October 1941.

of the German army, the Soviet Union had not been defeated in the expected four months. Sabotage and partisan operations behind German lines were increasing, and the Germans were forced to implement even harsher methods to keep occupied areas under their control. This may have led Hitler to take his frustrations out on the Jews. The killings by mass shooting

increased at a ferocious pace. Many volunteers from the Baltic States and Ukraine joined the *Einsatzgruppen* and strengthened it. In September 1941, came perhaps the most notorious revenge killing by German forces. After the third largest city, Kiev, had fallen in September, a massive explosion killed many German soldiers in the Continental Hotel in the city. As a reprisal, 33,771 Jews were taken to a ravine just outside the city and shot. Two years later, the corpses were dug up and burned in a desperate attempt to destroy the evidence of the crime.

Although all Jews were targeted for execution, in practice, some were used as slave labor. For these people, the threat of death was always present either from the guards' brutality, from disease, or from being worked or starved to death.

During the first wave of killings, from June 1941 to April 1942, some 750,000 Soviet Jews were probably murdered. An additional 1.5 million were killed in the second wave from 1942 to 1943.

The date that the decision was made to exterminate all of Europe's Jews is not certain. Documents about this are rare. Hitler probably gave the order verbally and expected Goering and Himmler to prepare the detailed plan and then ensure that it was carried out.

On January 20, 1942, a conference took place at a country house on the shores of Lake Wannsee, near Berlin. Reinhard Heydrich (head of the SS *Gestapo*, or secret police) chaired the Wannsee Conference. The object of the discussions was to coordinate the different government departments toward one single aim—the destruction of Europe's 11 million Jews. Heydrich told the delegates that Goering had asked to see the draft project for the Final Solution. The emigration and evacuation of the Jews had been just one step in the plan. Murder or extermination was never mentioned in the minutes of the meeting, but it is believed that everyone there would have known what the "Final Solution" actually involved. This term is believed to have meant that Europe's Jewish population would be murdered in the death camps.

German **Einsatzgruppen** *firing squads round up Soviet Jewish women in the Moldovian Republic in September 1941.*

SPEECH

"I hereby charge you with making all the necessary preparations with regard to organisational, technical, and material matters for bringing about a complete solution of the Jewish question within the German sphere of influence in Europe … I request you further send me, in the near future, an overall plan covering the organisational, technical, and material measures necessary for the accomplishment of the final solution of the Jewish question which we desire."

Speech from Goering to Heydrich, July 31, 1941.

The concentration camps

The attempted murder of all European Jews was organized with ruthless efficiency and carried out with the most advanced scientific and technological skills. Deportations to Eastern Europe began in all Nazi-occupied areas in 1939. Germany put pressure on the governments of their allies to do the same. Some, such as France, complied; others, such as

The Hungarian government had at first refused to deport its Jews, but by 1944, it finally gave into German pressure. Here Jewish children are being rounded up.

Hungary and Italy, resisted before they were finally forced to agree. Denmark smuggled virtually all of its Jewish population (about 7,000 people) out of the country to the safety of neutral Sweden.

The Jews were constantly deceived; they were told that they would be "resettled" in the east of Europe. The truth was that those judged "useless to the German war effort" were killed when they arrived at the camps. A smaller number were selected for forced labor and the remainder were rounded up into ghettos.

Gas had been used in the Euthanasia Program and the SS chose it again as the most efficient way to kill Jews and other unwanted ethnic and social groups. The doctors and scientists who had carried out the killing of the mentally and physically disabled were drafted into the program.

The first death camp was set up at Chelmno in Poland in 1941. The victims were killed in mobile gas vans using exhaust gas (carbon monoxide), which was fed back into the sealed vans through rubber hoses. A forest clearing, 3 miles (2 km) from Chelmno, had been prepared to receive the bodies. Later, a permanent gas chamber was set up. By the time the retreating Germans destroyed the camp in March 1943, some 140,000 Jews, gypsies, and Poles had been murdered there.

Other concentration camps in Poland became designated death camps—Treblinka, Belzec, Sobibor, Majdanek, and Auschwitz-Birkenau. Jews transported into the camps were crammed into closed cattle trucks where there were two buckets for toilets and no water or food. Once they arrived at the camps, the survivors were hurried out of the trucks by shouting guards, and SS doctors made a quick selection. The elderly, children, and mothers with children were sent straight to the gas chambers. They were taken to what they thought were shower rooms and told to remove their clothes and shoes. Then the doors were closed and carbon monoxide was pumped into the room. The Jewish death brigade (*Sonderkommando*) were forced to pull the bodies out after 30 minutes. Vast crematoria burned the bodies and the ashes were scattered.

In November 1943, Himmler wrote to Otto Globocnik, the SS police chief who had overseen the killing of the Polish Jews, to express his thanks "*and appreciation for the great and unique service which you have performed for the whole German people.*"

Buchenwald concentration camp was liberated in April 1945. Although this was not an extermination camp, 63,500 prisoners died of brutality and starvation.

Auschwitz-Birkenau

Auschwitz-Birkenau was not the only death camp, but it was the most infamous. Originally, it had been created as a concentration camp for Polish prisoners. By 1941, it had grown to an enormous forced labor camp for Soviet prisoners of war. By the late summer of 1941, Himmler told the camp commandant, Rudolph Hoess, that it was to be the main camp for exterminating Jews. Hoess was a fanatical Nazi who had joined the party in 1924 and the SS in 1934. He carried out his orders with great enthusiasm. He tested a new gassing agent, Zyklon B (pellets of Prussic acid), and was "delighted" with the results for it reduced the killing time by half.

The system of mass murder was further streamlined. Freight wagons arrived at a railroad platform between Auschwitz I and Auschwitz II-Birkenau. They were met by an SS doctor, who ordered some of the prisoners to be sent to work and others to death. The old, sick, and mothers with children were immediately sent to the gas chambers. Only about 30 percent were kept as workers. The SS and many major businesses made a fortune by exploiting this slave labor.

Prisoners were forced to wear different badges to indicate why they were in the camp, for example, homosexuals were required to wear pink triangles. Fed on a starvation diet of watery soup and bread, and punished brutally for small offenses, prisoners rarely survived more than three to four months.

Some Auschwitz prisoners were chosen for medical experiments. They were injected with chemicals and given massive doses of radiation. The purpose of these tests was to find a means of mass sterilization. Many died or suffered terrible aftereffects from the tests. By 1944, most Jews in

Prisoners in the camps were forced to wear badges. The yellow star was for Jews and the red triangle was for Czech political prisoners.

Jewish women, with their heads shaved, are marched away at Auschwitz. Within two hours of arriving, most would have been killed in the gas chambers.

German-occupied Europe had perished. Apart from the Danish Jews, the Hungarian Jews had also escaped because their government had protected them. This protection was not to last, however. In the spring of 1944, Adolf Eichmann arrived in the Hungarian capital, Budapest, to arrange the transportation of the surviving Jews. In less than a month, 289,000 Jews were transported from Hungary and most were killed on arrival at the death camps.

On November 2, 1944, Himmler gave the order for the exterminations to stop. The Soviet forces were advancing on the Eastern Front and the Nazis were desperately attempting to remove all traces of the death camps. Those prisoners that had survived were forced to march back to Germany. Many died on the march.

Jews, homosexuals, and many Poles and Soviets (possibly as many as 25 million) had been killed. Other victims included gypsies, Jehovah's Witnesses, criminals, and disabled people. It is estimated that 500,000 European gypsies were murdered. Up to 15,000 homosexuals were sent to camps and 40,000 criminals were killed. Around 200,000 disabled people were killed by the Nazis.

The Nuremberg Trials 1945–6

At the end of the war, the Allies were determined to punish the Nazi leaders for their crimes. Held in Germany, the Nuremberg Trials were an attempt by the Allies to show that leaders of countries who committed terrible crimes should be subject to the law, like anyone else. An International Military Tribunal, with judges from Britain, France, the U.S., and Soviet Union, charged 24 leading Nazis with:

- Crimes against peace
- Crimes against humanity
- War crimes
- Planning to commit the crimes in the charges above.

Some Nazi leaders—Hitler, Goebbels, and Himmler among them—had already committed suicide in 1945. At the end of the trial, 12 Nazis were found guilty and sentenced to hang, seven were given prison sentences, and the remainder were found "not guilty."

Other Nazis were brought to trial later, but many were acquitted or received light sentences. Some Nazis had escaped to South America, such as Doctor Josef Mengele, who had conducted experiments on camp prisoners. Other Nazis were caught. Most spectacularly, in 1960, Adolf Eichmann was apprehended and kidnapped by the Israeli secret service and then flown to Jerusalem for trial. He was hanged for war crimes.

The Nuremberg Trials were an attempt to punish the leading Nazis for the Holocaust. They were also meant to send a warning to other countries to behave according to humanitarian standards.

The Allied leaders were determined to punish leading Nazis, some of whom were put on trial at Nuremberg in Germany in 1945.

TIMELINE

1933
January — Adolf Hitler is appointed chancellor of Germany.

1934
April — Heinrich Himmler is appointed as the head of the SS.

1935
September — Nuremberg anti-Semitic laws are passed.

1936
August — The Olympic Games are held in Berlin.

1937
January — Jews are banned from professional occupations, including teaching.

1938
March — *Anschluss*. All anti-Semtic laws against the Jews in Germany are extended to the Austrian Jews.

August — Nazis force Jewish women to add "Sarah" to their names and Jewish men "Israel" on all legal documents.

November — Extreme violence during *Kristallnacht* takes place against the Jews.

1939
September — Germany invades Poland. WWII begins.

1940
June — France is occupied by the Nazis.

October — Anti-Jewish laws are passed in France.

November — The Warsaw ghetto in Poland is created containing 400,000 Jews.

1941
January — Polish Jews living near Warsaw are deported to the ghetto.

June — Soviet Union is invaded by the Germans. The *Einsatzgruppen* units begin the mass murder of Jewish victims.

1942
January — The Wannsee Conference plans the extermination of all Jews under German control.

July — A Jewish resistance fighting organization is established in Warsaw.

1943
February — The German 6th Army surrenders at Stalingrad.

April — The Jewish uprising in the Warsaw ghetto.

September — The Danish underground rescues 7,000 Jews, who escape to Sweden.

1944
June — Allied troops land in France.

November — Himmler orders an end to the gas chambers at Auschwitz.

1945
April — Allied troops enter the concentration camps. Hitler commits suicide.

May — Germany surrenders to the Allies.

November–October — The Nuremberg War Trials.

1962
May — Adolf Eichmann is executed for war crimes following his trial in Israel in 1961.

GLOSSARY

Anschluss
Union of Germany and Austria.

Anti-Semitism
Hatred of the Jews.

Aryan
Germanic races believed by the Nazis to be the superior race.

Barbarossa
German plan to attack the Soviet Union and the Soviet people.

Einsatzcommando
An individual detachment of the *Einsatzgruppen*.

Einsatzgruppen
Action squads. SS units responsible for the murder of inferior racial groups.

Eugenics
A so-called science of races.

Euthanasia
The act or practice of killing terminally sick or injured individuals for reasons of mercy.

Final Solution
A phrase used by the Nazis to describe their program for the extermination of the Jews.

Fuhrer
The Nazi leader—Adolf Hitler.

Gestapo
Secret State Police.

Ghetto
An area of a town where Jews were forced to live.

Hebrew
A Semitic language originating in Israel from around the tenth century B.C.

Holocaust
The term used after the war for the murder of some six million Jews.

Judaism
The religion of the Jewish people.

Judenraat
Jewish councils.

Kristallnacht
The campaign of Nazi attacks on synagogues, Jewish property, and the murder of Jews in Germany 1938.

Lebensraum
Living space. Conquering Eastern Europe for German colonization.

Mandate
When a territory is entrusted to a country to administer until it is ready for independence.

Mein Kampf
The title of Hitler's autiobiography translates as "My Struggle," and the book explains his racial and political ideas.

NSDAP
Nationalsozialistische Deutsche Arbeiterpartei— National Socialist German Workers' Party— the Nazis.

Pogroms
Attacks on Jews in eastern Europe.

Rabbi
The leader of a Jewish congregation.

Reichstag
The German parliament.

Shtetls
Jewish towns in eastern Europe.

SS
Schutzstaffel—Protection Squad. Nazi elite organization that controlled Nazi Germany.

Volk
A people and nation with an ethnic and cultural identity.

Volley
Simultaneous shooting of weapons.

Weimar Republic
The name of the republican government in Germany between 1919 and 1933.

Yiddish
A mixed language of German and Hebrew.

Zionists
Jewish settlers in Palestine.

FURTHER INFORMATION

FURTHER READING

Nonfiction books

Anne Frank: The Diary of a Young Girl by Anne Frank, Bantam, 1993

Days of Change: The Holocaust by Valerie Bodden, Creative Education, 2007

Flowers on the Wall by Miriam Nerlove, Margaret K Elderberry Books, 1996

From Prejudice to Genocide by Carrie Supple, Trentham Books, 2007

In My Pocket by Dorrith Sim, Harcourt, 1997

My Secret Camera: Life in the Lodz Ghetto by Mendel Grossman and Frank Smith, Francis Lincoln Ltd, 2008

Schindler's List by Thomas Keneally, Touchstone, 1993

The Holocaust Causes by Patricia Levy, Raintree Steck-Vaughn, 2001

The Pianist by Wladyslaw Szpilman, Picador, 2002

Fiction books

Boat of Stone by Maureen Earl, Permanent Press, 1993

The Boy in Striped Pajamas by John Boyne, David Fickling Books, 2007

Web Sites

Due to the changing nature of Internet links, Rosen Publishing has developed an online list of Web Sites related to the subject of this book. This site is regularly updated. Please use this link to access this list:
http://www.rosenlinks.com/dww/holo

PLACES TO VISIT

Florida Holocaust Museum,
55 5th Street South, St. Petersburg, FL 33701

United States Holocaust Memorial Museum,
100 Raoul Wallenberg Place, SW Washington, DC 20024-2126

INDEX

Numbers in **bold** refer to illustrations.

Anschluss 29
anti-Jewish legislation 26–7, 28–9
anti-Semitism 5, 6–7, 8–9, 10–11, 12, 14–15, **15**, 18–19, **19**, 21, 22–3, **23**, 29
Aryan beliefs 9, 11, 12, **15**, 20, **27**
Auschwitz-Birkenau **5**, 21, 40, 42–3, **43**

Bismarck, Otto von 7
Black Death 8

Chamberlain, Houston Stewart 11
Chelmno 40
communists 17, 36
concentration camps 5, **5**, 21, 31, 40–41, **41**, 42–3

Der Stürmer 23
disabled people 4, 20, 43
Dreyfus, Captain 7
Duhring, Eugene 10

Eichmann, Adolf 29, 43, 44
Einsatzcommandos 36
Einsatzgruppen **32**, 33, 36, 38, **39**
Enabling Act 17
eugenics 9, 21
execution squads *also see Einsatzgruppen* 5, 36, 37
extermination policy 20, **20**, 21, **32**, 33, 36, 37, 38, 39, 40–41, 42–3, **43**

Final Solution, the 5, 39
French Revolution 8–9

genocide 4–5
German
    conquest of Europe 32–3, **33**
    culture 10
    economy 14, 15, 16, 22, 24, 28
    history 10
    nationalism 10, 13, 14
ghettos 34–5, 34, 36, 37, 40
Globocnik, Otto 41
Gobineau, Count Joseph Arthur de 9

Goebbels, Josef 18, **18**, 30, 44
Goering, Hermann 28, 31, 38, 39
gypsies 4, 21, 33, 40

Heydrich, Reinhard 32, 39
Himmler, Heinrich **16**, 17, 31, 38, 41, 42, 43, 44
Hindenburg, President 16, 17
Hitler, Adolf **9**, 12–13, 14, 16, 17, 22–3, 28, 30, 31, 32, 33, 36, 38, 44
Hitler Putsch **12**, 13
Hitler Youth 19
Hoess, Rudolph 42
homosexuals 21, 42, 43

Israel 6, 8, 29, 44

Jehovah's Witnesses 4, 43
Jews
    and communism 14
    culture and beliefs 6–7, **6**, 8
    deportation of 35, 40, **40**, 43
    emigration of 24–5, 29, 31, 32, 39
    in Eastern Europe 6, 9
    in western Europe 7, 9
    persecution of 4–5, 6, 8–9, **8**, 19, 22–3, **22**, 24–5, **24**, 26–7, 29, 30–31, 38, **39**
    population distribution **4**
    resistance of 35, **36**, 37
    wealth and influence 14
Judenraat 34

Kristallnacht 30–31, **30**

Law of the Restoration of the Professional Civil Service 23
lebensraum 20, 33, 36
Leibknecht, Karl 14
Lubbe, Marinus van der 17
Luxemburg, Rosa 14

Mein Kampf 9, 13, **13**
Mengele, Dr. Josef 44

National Socialist German Workers' Party (Nazi Party) 13, 15, 17, 18, 19, 22, 28, 31
Nazis **12**, 14, 16–17, 18–19, **18**, 19, 20, 21, 24–5, 26, 33, 36, 44

Nuremburg Trials 44, **44**

Olympic Games (1936) 28, **28**
Operation Barbarossa 36, 38

Palestine 6–7, 25
Papen, Franz von 16
Poland and Polish people 32, 33, 34, 37, 40, 42, 43
propaganda 18–19, **19**, **23**, 26, **27**, 28, **28**, **29**, 30
Protocols of the Elders of Zion, The 14, **14**

racism 4, 9, **29**
Reichstag 16–17
Ritter, Dr. Robert 21
Rumkovski, Chaim 35

SA (*Sturm-Abteilung*) 22, **22**, 23, 31
shtetls 6
slave labor 38, 40, 42
Soviet Union and Soviet people 5, 33, 36, 38, 43
SS (*Schutzstaffel*) 17, 29, 33, 36, 38, 40, 41, 42
sterilization policy 20–21, 42
Streicher, Julius **26**, 28

Torah, the 6

volk 10, 20

Wagner, Richard 10–11, **11**
Wannsee Conference 39
Warsaw Uprising 35
Weimar Government 12, 15
World War I 6, 14
World War II 4–5

Yiddish 6

Zionists 6–7

OPELIKA HIGH LIBRARY

OHS

OPELIKA HIGH LIBRARY